C000051257

# The Forward Book
# of Poetry 2000

FORWARD PUBLISHING
LONDON

First published in Great Britain by
Forward Publishing · 84-86 Regent Street · London W1R 6DD
in association with
Faber and Faber · 3 Queen Square · London WC1N 3AU

ISBN 0 571 20220 9 (paperback)

Compilation copyright © Forward Publishing 1999
For copyright on individual poems see Acknowledgements page 9
Foreword copyright © Simon Armitage 1999
Front cover illustration by Andy Lovell

Reprographics by Graphic Ideas Studios Ltd
London

Printed by Redwood Books Ltd
Kennet House · Kennet Way · Trowbridge · Wilts BA14 8RN

A CIP catalogue reference for this book
is available at the British Library.

To Aaron Rose

# Preface

WELCOME TO THE EIGHTH FORWARD BOOK OF POETRY, an anthology
of poems entered for the 1999 Forward Poetry Prizes. As always, the
judges' selection gives a fascinating picture of contemporary poetry and
contemporary life. I hope that both enthusiasts and novices will find it
as intriguing and satisfying as its predecessors.

It has been an eventful year for poetry – beginning with the death of
Ted Hughes, the Poet Laureate, just two weeks after he received the
Forward Prize for his best-selling *Birthday Letters*, and ending with the
appointment of a new Laureate, Andrew Motion.

The theme of this year's National Poetry Day is the nation's
favourite song lyric. Songwriters and lyricists as poets? Why not?
By making a link between songs and poems, we hope to help even
confirmed sceptics understand how approachable and accessible
contemporary poetry can be.

In creating *The Forward Book of Poetry* and its partner in verse,
National Poetry Day, we at the Forward Poetry Trust have received
help and finance from a number of sources. We would like to thank
Gordon Kerr at Waterstone's and Jeffery Tolman and Peter Cunard
at Tolman Cunard.

We would also like to thank the poetry commandos who have helped
to make our poetry festivities complete: our judges for this year's prize
(Simon Armitage, Helen Dunmore, Penelope Shuttle, Erica Wagner
and John Walsh); our partners at the BBC; The Poetry Society; Colman
Getty; Faber and Faber; and everyone at Forward Publishing.

Thank you all, and happy reading.

William Sieghart

# Foreword

CAN ONE POEM really be said to be better or worse than another? Yes, is my own view, and there would be little or no point sitting on a panel of judges without a firm belief in the meritocracy of writing. The good stuff will come to the top, and when it does, it should be recognised and rewarded.

Let's take, for the sake of a ludicrous comparison, the motor car. One vehicle might be praised for its economy, one for its speed, another for its comfort, another for its design, and so on. Some cars are good cars, for a variety of different reasons, and some cars are classics. Some will always be rubbish. Poetry is a more sensitive issue; it often deals with feelings, and is seen in a subjective light. But the truth is that some poems have acceleration, some have style, some have power, some have high technical specification, and some make important statements about environmental consciousness, unleaded petrol and the planet's finite resources. In comparison, other poems are left standing.

If that sounds harsh, then I should also say that the most satisfying aspect of the Forward Prize is its democratic nature. Not only does the Prize consider work by Poet Laureates, Nobel prizewinners and other well-established authors, but it does so alongside the work of poets who might be publishing for the very first time, in the most obscure magazines and journals. In that respect, the Forward Prize attempts to give a fair hearing to the whole chorus of poetic utterance, from those whose poetry practises a kind of Masonic handshake with literary criticism, to those whose poems are more like sleeve-notes, or souvenirs of their work as performers and entertainers. The inclusion of poets born or living outside Britain, who publish in this country, is a further reflection of the eclecticism and pluralism that characterises contemporary poetry, and is a welcome addition to the diversity of language and attitude on display in this book.

Some introductions to anthologies can take on a depressing, hand-wringing tone, as if there were an ongoing need to justify the very existence of poetry. Like a church with its empty pews, poetry is described as a kind of charity case of worthy cause, and such introductions usually conclude with heartfelt statements as to poetry's sacred importance and fundamental value. Instead, I'm taking the view that people reading this book will be doing so out of pleasure rather than guilt, are well aware of contemporary poetry's vitality, and might be interested to learn how the contents of this volume were chosen.

In terms of the prizes for the three different categories, all five judges came up with their own selections – a process which resulted in a healthy measure of variation and a satisfying degree of coincidence. The final, official shortlists, were arrived at through lengthy discussion, followed by an election process that included the single transferable vote as well as some aspect of proportional representation. Thanks are due to Margot Weale of Colman Getty for her skills in differential calculus and her ability to decipher tube tickets doubling as ballot papers.

In The Best Collection category, the five shortlisted volumes almost seemed to choose themselves. Two of those books happen to be published by Oxford University Press, and it's irresistible not to think of this as a two-fingered cheerio to a publisher that recently chose to discontinue its contemporary poetry list for no good reason whatsoever.

In The Best First Collection class, we chose from writers who have already made something of a name for themselves, as well as from poets who seem to have arrived from nowhere. A lot of good writing has made it between the covers of a full-length book for the first time this year.

The Best Individual Poem section is slightly complicated by the fact that entries are pre-selected by editors of the various periodicals and newspapers in which the poems first appeared. Picking five poems from such a wide-ranging selection is almost an impossible task, and is also the most fun.

Of The Other Poems contained within the anthology, each of the judges selected a bundle of their favourites, and in they went – not a recognised editorial technique, but a fair one in terms of representing our different tastes.

The winners of the Forward Prizes, at the moment of writing this, are yet to be decided. And just to sound a note of caution, it's important, I reckon, to think of the Prize as a system of awards, rather than viewing the whole thing as some sort of competition – the literary version of Crufts. When the best poets sit down with their pens or laptops, they aren't even thinking of books or publishing contracts, they're thinking only of the poem. From a personal point of view, I've now experienced the Forward Prize from every angle: as a judge, as chair, as a person who climbed on to the podium to trouser a cheque, as a drunk spectator at the prize-giving, and memorably, as a loser. On that last occasion, it would have helped to see the Prize for what it is – a way of celebrating and circulating what is deemed to be the best poetry written in a particular year. A parade, rather than a race for the line.

Even in the cruel world of good poems and bad ones, there are no losers in the year 2000 *Forward Book of Poetry*, only a number of contenders, and three winners waiting to be announced.

Simon Armitage

# Acknowledgements

Annemarie Austin · SWADDLED · *Door upon Door* · Bloodaxe Books

Matthew Barton · THE GULF VETERAN'S WIFE DOESN'T FORSEE A LOT ·
   *Learning to Row* · Peterloo Poets

John Burnside · THE ASYLUM DANCE · Agenda

Sue Butler · FOLKLORE · *Via Leeds to Lake Ladoga* · Redbeck Press

Matthew Caley · COLANDER MAN · EIGHT WAYS OF LOOKING AT LAKES ·*Thirst* ·
   Slow Dancer Poetry

Ciaran Carson · THE WIND THAT SHAKES THE BARLEY · *The Twelfth of Never* ·
   Picador

Caroline Carver · –HORSE UNDER WATER– · National Poetry Competition

Kate Clanchy · THE NATURAL HISTORY MUSEUM · WAR POETRY · *Samarkand* ·
   Picador

Gillian Clarke · HORSE GODDESS · *Five Fields* · Carcanet

Robert Crawford · ZERO · Poetry Review

Amanda Dalton · NEST · STRONG HANDS · *How to Disappear* · Bloodaxe Books

Marcia Douglas · ELECTRICITY COMES TO COCOA BOTTOM ·
   *Electricity Comes to Cocoa Bottom* · Peepal Tree

Nick Drake · IN MEMORY OF VINCENT COX · THE SINGLE SHOES OF SPAIN ·
   *The Man in the White Suit* · Bloodaxe Books

Jane Draycott · AMATEUR RADIO · BRAVING THE DARK · *Prince Rupert's Drop* ·
   Oxford University Press

Carol Ann Duffy · ANNE HATHAWAY · THE DEVIL'S WIFE · *The World's Wife* ·
   Picador

Pamela Gillilan · THREE WAYS TO A SILK SHIRT · *The Rashomon Syndrome* ·
   Bloodaxe Books

Paul Groves · A HIGH ROOM OFF SPITALGASSE · *Eros and Thanatos* · Seren

Mark Halliday · *WHANG* EDITORIAL POLICY · Poetry Review

Sophie Hannah · NEXT DOOR DESPISED · *Leaving and Leaving You* · Carcanet

Ian Harrow · BIOGRAPHICAL · *Polemos* · Eperon Press

David Hart · LATE · New Welsh Review 42

W N Herbert · FIRST FIT · *The Laurelude* · Bloodaxe Books

Michael Hofmann · LAST WALK · *Approximately Nowhere* · Faber and Faber

Jackie Kay · CROWN AND COUNTRY · *Off Colour* · Bloodaxe Books

August Kleinzahler · SUNDAY MORNING · *Green Sees Things in Waves* ·
    Faber and Faber

Michael Laskey · HOME MOVIES · *The Tightrope Wedding* ·
    Smith/Doorstop Books

Aidan Mathews · TOTAL IMMERSION · *According to the Small Hours* · Cape

Roger McGough · THE WAY THINGS ARE · *The Way Things Are* · Penguin

Robert Minhinnick · TWENTY-FIVE LAMENTS FOR IRAQ · PN Review

Andrew Motion · SERENADE · Times Literary Supplement

Paul Muldoon · HAY · WIRE · *Hay* · Faber and Faber

Les Murray · TRAVELS WITH JOHN HUNTER · PN Review

Stephanie Norgate · THE WHEEDLING MAN · *Fireclay* · Smith/Doorstop Books

Christopher North · THE DOG · HARD TIMES · *A Mesh of Wires* ·
    Smith/Doorstop Books

Bernard O'Donoghue · HERMES · Times Literary Supplement

Pascale Petit · FOSSILING · *Heart of a Deer* · Enitharmon

Peter Porter ·To MY GRANDAUGHTERS SWEEPING SPELSBURY CHURCH ·
    *Collected Poems 2* · Oxford University Press

Sheenagh Pugh · THE TORMENTED CENSOR · *Stonelight* · Seren

Peter Reading · AXIOMATIC · *Ob.* · Bloodaxe Books

Jo Shapcott · MANDRAKE PIE · THETIS · *My Life Asleep* · Oxford University Press

Michael Symmons Roberts · THE EEL GATHERERS · *Raising Sparks* · Cape

George Szirtes · BACKWATERS: NORFOLK FIELDS · The Rialto

R S Thomas · BLACKBIRD · Agenda

Adam Thorpe · PICKINGS · *From the Neanderthal* · Cape

Jeffrey Wainwright · THE HUMANE HOUSE · *Out of the Air* · Carcanet

Andrew Waterhouse · ONE DAY IN LATE ADOLESCENCE · Smiths Knoll 18

Robert Wells · FIVE SKETCHES · *Lusus* · Carcanet

Christiania Whitehead · ANGELS · GRIP ·*The Garden of Slender Trust* ·
    Bloodaxe Books

Gerard Woodward · THE HANDSTAND SUMMER · *Island to Island* ·
    Chatto & Windus

# Contents

The Best Collection Poems

# Kate Clanchy

## THE NATURAL HISTORY MUSEUM

They are glassed and boxed like childhood,
the dead creatures in their pastoral
dance: the grinning fox and pouting squirrel,
the ferrets in their stiff quadrille. Parents nod
and watch their children watch the bloodshed
always about to happen: the wee mouse
cower, the wildcat locked in a pointless
leap. It was Bosch, I think, who painted
the Cat padding into Eden with a small beast
limp in her mouth. A child smiles. Her father
aims a camera. He shoots, and does not ask
what the half-silvered hare asserts,
stopped on the cusp of change, forever
almost escaping, kicking his heels at the dark.

## War Poetry

The class has dropped its books. The janitor's
disturbed some wasps, broomed the nest
straight off the roof. It lies outside, exotic
as a fallen planet, a burst city of the poor;
its newsprint halls, its ashen, tiny rooms
all open to the air. The insects' buzz
is low-key as a smart machine. They group,
regroup, in stacks and coils, advance
and cross like pulsing points on radar screens.

And though the boys have shaven heads
and football strips, and would, they swear,
enlist at once, given half a chance,
march down Owen's darkening lanes
to join the lads and stuff the Boche –
they don't rush out to pike the nest,
or lap the yard with grapeshot faces.
They watch the wasps through glass,
silently, abashed, the way we all watch war.

# Jane Draycott

## Amateur Radio

Fishing in the rolling dark, they cast their calls
onto the blind waves. C Q, seek you, seek you out.
Like ropes, or an arm flung out in a dream.

The ether licks at their call-signs and swallows them
whole. After such a journey near to drowning
in the earth's white air there's nobody won't let you in.

Sat together with strangers, the fat sparks fly.
Golf One Delta Zulu is beaming towards the East,
reliving the magic of hot valves and long black ebonite rods.

Seek you, seek you out. No politics or religion by law.
Appel général, appel général. I am being interfered with.
Fine business old man. George is telling us about his bees.

I am seriously troubled by static. You may make remarks
of a personal character. I am being interfered with. I'm troubled.
Fine business. We're still dead on seven three five.

And they all listen out on the singing arc for a heart-beat
of morse, for a pulse in the chhh chhh chhh. Like blood
through a stethoscope, or the sea in their ears.

BRAVING THE DARK

*in memory of my brother Nigel and for the staff of London Lighthouse*

I   Search

Passive, your glove allows me to enter
its five black-soft tunnels:
the tips however remained uninhabited,
your fingers having been longer than mine.

The words you typed and left, expecting to return,
file out across their electronic lawn.
I caress them with the cursor, like a medium
stroking the table at a seance.

At your pain on the answerphone tape my voice
sticks, as at the gaps in a linguaphone lesson.
In tears, I sort the wafers of your clothes for friends–
straightjacketed in card you watch, and seem unmoved.

At last day buckles and, awake in bed, I find you:
the deadweight limbs we turned two-hourly
and powdered to protect your baffled skin
become my own, crook'd flat along the sheet

and from the soft lame triangle that your mouth became
you breathe our childhood out upon my pillow.
Wearing the features of our father,
your frightened face sleeps inside mine.


II   Dream

The Vicar arrives by rowing-boat,
vampire-stalks our wet front path
and batlike settles out his cloak
for The Consolation of the Bereaved

(flashback to our mother's funeral
when we remarked how very like a piece of theatre
funerals are, as his hand webbed out
a fraction on his Book of Common Prayer).

His head is tortoising out to kiss me.
I am trying to explain my disinclination
to dance, when you appear suddenly from the lounge,
perfectly whole, to save me.

Outside the door the road is dry again,
the vicar desubstantiated. At last
we're on our own and you can tell me
how it is that you're not really dead after all.


III  Piano-movers

They came like ambulance-men
in mufti, thick-soled
and trained to be careful.

*Why then must he go in red blankets,*
*he had played it to know,*
*and the virus allowed to ride inside?*

In one gentle tackle they had the legs
from under it. Winded, it blurted
strange harmonies and going down was still.

*He had dreamt the last test*
*had come negative, though upon the keys*
*his Hansel-and-Gretel fingers unwove the fantastic lie.*

Easing it deadweight
shoulder, they tucked the flung elbow flat
and pulled deftly on blankets and straps.

*'Can't you change it?'*
*he'd asked of the strangers*
*who tended his body, but failed to reply.*

Invisible neighbours watched its wheeled
passage, bumped prone down the front path
between unknown bearers.


IV   Mahogany

Pressing down in twos and threes
the slack teeth of the piano's smile
I try to conjure you,
your hip knuckling against mine
for just one more shambling duet.

You do not appear: I seal
the mute mahogany. Propped
on the music-rest I read
the notes you ink-embroidered
in a song for me: Lullay, and hush.

Scattered families of notes fragment
and shimmy above their own reflections.
It's a Lovely Day Tomorrow,
you used to sing
at gilt kosher soirées. Evening
lays out along the tautened strings:
the black silk thread
along the edge of your lapel
is as clear as your face
as in the dark you stand to sing
your heart out.

# Carol Ann Duffy

ANNE HATHAWAY

*"Item I gyve unto my wief my second best bed..."*
*(from Shakespeare's will).*

The bed we loved in was a spinning world
of forests, castles, torchlight, clifftops, seas
where he would dive for pearls. My lover's words
were shooting stars which fell to earth as kisses
on these lips; my body now a softer rhyme
to his, now echo, assonance; his touch
a verb dancing in the centre of a noun.
Some nights, I dreamed he'd written me, the bed
a page beneath his writer's hands. Romance
and drama played by touch, by scent, by taste.
In the other bed, the best, our guests dozed on,
dribbling their prose. My living laughing love–
I hold him in the casket of my widow's head
as he held me upon that next best bed.

# The Devil's Wife

## 1  Dirt

The Devil was one of the men at work.
Different. Fancied himself. Looked at the girls
in the office as though they were dirt. Didn't flirt.
Didn't speak. Was sarcastic and rude if he did.
I'd stare him out, chewing my gum, insolent, dumb.
I'd lie on my bed at home, on fire for him.

I scowled and pouted and sneered. I gave
as good as I got till he asked me out. In his car,
he put two fags in his mouth and lit them both.
He bit my breast. His language was foul. He entered me.
We're the same, he said, That's it. I swooned in my soul.
We drove to the woods and he made me bury a doll.

I went mad for the sex. I won't repeat what we did.
We gave up going to work. It was either the woods
or looking at playgrounds, fairgrounds. Coloured lights
in the rain. I'd walk around on my own. He tailed.
I felt like this: Tongue of stone. Two black slates
for eyes. Thumped wound of a mouth. Nobody's Mam.


## 2  Medusa

I flew in my chains over the wood where we'd buried
the doll. I know it was me who was there.
I know I carried the spade. I know I was covered in mud.
But I cannot remember how or when or precisely where.

Nobody liked my hair. Nobody liked how I spoke.
He held my heart in his fist and he squeezed it dry.
I gave the cameras my Medusa stare.
I heard the judge summing-up. I didn't care.

I was left to rot. I was locked up, double-locked.
I know they chucked the key. It was nowt to me.
I wrote to him every day in our private code.
I thought in twelve, fifteen, we'd be out on the open road.

But life, they said, means life. Dying inside.
The Devil was evil, mad, but I was the Devil's wife
Which made me worse. I howled in my cell.
If the Devil was gone then how could this be hell?


3   Bible

I said No not me I didn't I couldn't I wouldn't.
Can't remember no idea not in the room.
Get me a Bible honestly promise you swear.
I never not in a million years it was him.

I said Send me a lawyer a vicar a priest.
Send me a TV crew send me a journalist.
Can't remember not in the room. Send me
a shrink where's my MP send him to me.

I said Not fair not right not on not true
not like that. Didn't see didn't know didn't hear.
Maybe this maybe that not sure not certain maybe.
Can't remember no idea it was him it was him.

Can't remember no idea not in the room.
No idea can't remember not in the room.


4   Night

In the long fifty-year night,
these are the words that crawl out of the wall:
Suffer. Monster. Burn in hell.

When morning comes,
I will finally tell.

Amen.


5   Appeal

If I'd been stoned to death
If I'd been hung by the neck
If I'd been shaved and strapped to the Chair
If an injection
If my peroxide head on the block
If my outstretched hands for the chop
If my tongue torn out at the root
If from ear to ear my throat
If a bullet a hammer a knife
If life means life means life means life

But what did I do to us all, to myself
When I was the Devil's wife?

# Paul Muldoon

## Hay

This much I know. Just as I'm about to make that right turn
off Province Line Road
I meet another beat-up Volvo
carrying a load

of hay. (More accurately, a bale of lucerne
on the roof rack,
a bale of lucerne or fescue or alfalfa.)
My hands are raw. I'm itching to cut the twine, to unpack

that hay-accordion, that hay-concertina.
It must be ten o'clock. There's still enough light
(not least from the glow

of the bales themselves) for a body to ascertain
that when one bursts, as now, something takes flight
from those hot and heavy box-pleats. This much, at least, I know.

## WIRE

As I roved out this morning at daybreak
I took a short cut
through the pine forest, following the high-tension wires
past the timber line
till I stumbled upon a makeshift hide or shooting-box
from which a command-wire seemed to run

intermittently along the ski-run
or fire-break.
I glanced into the hideout. A school lunch-box.
A pear so recently cut
I thought of Ceylon. A can of Valvoline.
Crocodile clips. Sri Lanka, I mean. A hank of wire

that might come in handy if ever I'd want to hot-wire
a motor and make a run
for the border. From just beyond my line
of vision I glimpsed something, or someone, break
cover for an instant. A shaved head, maybe, or a crew-cut.
Jumping up like a jack-in-the-box

before ducking back down. Then a distant raking through the
    gear-box
of a truck suddenly gone haywire
on this hillside of hillsides in Connecticut
brought back some truck on a bomb run,
brought back so much with which I'd hoped to break –
the hard-line

yet again refusing to toe the line,
the bullet and the ballot box,
the joy-ride, the jail-break,
Janet endlessly singing 'The Men behind the Wire',
the endless re-run
of Smithfield, La Mon, Enniskillen, of bodies cut

to ribbons as I heard the truck engine cut
and, you might have read as much between the lines,
ducked down here myself behind the hide. As if I myself were on
    the run.
The truck driver handing a box-
cutter, I'm sure, to the bald guy. A pair of real live wires.
I've listened to them all day now, torn between making a break

for it and their talk of the long run, the short term, of boxing
    clever,
fish or cut bait, make or break,
the end of the line, right down to the wire.

# Jo Shapcott

## MANDRAKE PIE

At home and abroad, we English brag about pie.
Our sailors bring home not just those heart-shaped boxes
crusted with little shells, but pie-cutters carved in doldrum days.

Implements of bone, one, two, or fabulously three-wheeled,
but always true, they allow fancy lattice-cutting back home
where no girl is marriageable until her pastry is so translucent

a sailor can read his tabloid right through it. Mandrake,
smelly, dangerous root of wonderful virtues, makes
the queen of pies, gives women babies and holds the wisdom

of the screaming dead. Pull your mandrake at dawn, double root
said to have grown from seeds of murderers put to death.
Ignore the shrieks as you tug and the scent that turns you on.

Bake it in the hottest oven you can get to make the air expand,
the pastry rise, as light as babies' breath. Ease the dough
into the tin, fill to the brim with the rough-chopped root,

and sprinkle with milk and water. Cover with pastry; seal
with a fork and then, and only then, may you lightly prick
the surface of your pie all over to let the screams escape.

## THETIS

No man can frighten me. Watch as I stretch
my limbs for the transformation, I'm laughing
to feel the surge of other shapes beneath my skin.
It's like this: here comes the full thrill of my art
as the picture of a variegated
lizard insinuates itself into my mind.
I extend my neck, lengthen fingers, push
down toes to find the form. My back begins
to undulate, the skin to gleam. I think
my soul has slithered with me into this
shape as real as the little, long tongue in my mouth,
as the sun on my back, as the skill in absolute stillness.
My name is Thetis Creatrix and you,
voyeur, if you looked a little closer, would see
the next ripples spread up my bloody tail, to bloom
through my spine as the bark begins to harden
over my trunk. Already I'm so much the oak
I lean everything towards the black oxygen
in the black air, I process delicious gases
through my personal chemistry, suck moisture
from the earth to a pulse so slow you can't detect it.
Next tigress. Low tremendous purrs start at the pit
of my stomach, I'm curving through long grass,
all sinew, in a body where tension
is the special joy and where the half-second
before a leap tells it all. Put out a paw
to dab a stone, an ant, a dead lamb. Life,
my life, is all play even up to the moment
when I'm tripped up, thrown down, bound,
raped until I bleed from my eyes,
beaten out of shape and forced to bring forth War.

*Thetis was a sea goddess who had the marvellous ability to change her shape.
Peleus was taught by Proteus the way to overcome her: to bind her and hold on
tightly whatever shape she took. The result of this forced union was Achilles.*

# The Best First Collection Poems

# Matthew Caley

## COLANDER MAN

Butterflies. Both holding metal ingots to his lobes
       or etched in blue-black ink upon his skin,
wild markings of the lunar-moth
       writhe upon his shin
and ankles. What isn't tattooed
       is pierced, spiked, gelled or cropped
–a crop-circle appeared mysteriously one night
       in the back of his haircut–
tie-dyed, crimped or lopped,

not to mention the topiary of sideboards
       and goatee beard. No, not to mention them.
Yet the day came when all this came undone.
       When, like a prospector
panning for precious stones
       -s he spat out all the little bits of dirt
and fool's gold
       from his eyelids, nostrils, earlobes, lips
and chin even, yes, his foreskin,

–as once disported
       by the esteemed Prince Consort–
and they fell to the floor
       like pond-ripples, clinking
to leave him porous
       as if peppered with grapeshot from a blunderbuss.
(Skin-grafts meant that the butterflies
       had their day and that all the dyes
ran to the one colour and melted.)

Next, he discarded the buckles, bibs, straps,
        bull-dog clips and bullet-belts,
stepping out of the dropped hoop
        of his clothes –leaving them to the moths–
like a new-born thing.
        Then he ran outside to the breeze
and pavement-slap. Out amongst
        the colour-coded traffic.
The wind blew through him and made music.

# Eight Ways Of Looking At Lakes

**1**
From afar, like Ishtar, aloof
on some spectacular limestone outcrop,
through binoculars. You'll be suffering from a headache
beyond the reach of *Aspirin*. It is a headache-coloured sky
and the lake itself is a grey headache, an undistinguished lozenge,
part of a panoramic, cinemascopic sweep,
but boring beneath the sky's distemper,
small.

**2**
Imagine yourself a minor Lakeland poet,
far from his sister's tussock, plucking an albatross, nursing the itch
of syphilis. With his laudanum-phial and, of course,
his vellum-bound volume of verse. Things can only
get better after this.
Or worse.

**3**
Close-up. In sunshine. With everything holiday-brochure bright,
airbrushed even. Even. Catch the surface-spangles, gyres, spirals,
silvery ring-pulls, rivets, all chainmail-linked and glinting. Think
of the importance of surfaces. The planes of people's faces.
Be satisfied with shallows. Here clouds are mountains,
mountains clouds and sheeted lakes, inscrutable, mirror both.
For the adventurous, dip your toe halfway
up your toenail. For the gifted – get walking.

**4***a*

Read W. H. Auden's *Lakes* [from *Bucolics*] and know all there is
   to know.
Almost. When you have finished, check the Ordinance Survey Map
of his face. Find solace in each fissure. Wallow.

4*b*

An ankle-deep paddle. We are 70% water ourselves. Little lopsided
waking lakes. Hardly amniotic. Hardly baptismal. Though
                                                watch out
for suddenly sepulchral doves that come and go
in a tin-flash. And don't forget your socks
busy sunbathing on the bank


5

Skinny-dipping. Let the salt support you. Think how many salt tears
would constitute a lake. That cold gasp as lakewater hits your groin.
Dippings, siftings, bits floating off. Your umbilical now knotted
and not in service. Sun-spangles on your cellulite
and your runny, foreshortened legs, thalidomide in rivulets.
Drift off, a jungle-raft to Samarkand and


6

have sex like waterbabies spawning in the spray.
The more professional can water-ski or analyse the wave-raked silt
replete with collective guilt and plastic goggles. Find the greeny-blue
bodies of underage boys and girls barely recognisable
from the local Echo or Star. Lapping darkness. The moiré effect
                                                of bubbles.
Deep, deep. You are diving too deep.


7

The one rule is 'everything ends'.
You now have a choice between the bottom or the bends.


8

This is the bottom. Grey-blue, billowing. Krakens, crud.
Long-missed Masons, rust. An underwater city of muffled bells
malingering beyond. Water or land. No-one can tell which is which.
When you finally set foot in Atlantis
its dust is dry to the touch.

# Amanda Dalton

## Nest

I'm building a nest in the garden
and watching my breath disappear
into splintered trees.
The sky is scratched and freezing;
birds are trapped in it.

I finger veins on damaged leaves
and put my ear to the cracked soil
but there's no pulse.
My nest will be of dead and aching things,
lined with my wedding dress,
decorated with our broken flowers.

I'll sing a marriage song behind my throat
where everything is cold and trapped.
Save me from losing my breath in the hard air.
Save me from screaming like birds
and wondering how things disappear.

I'm setting up home without you,
unpacking my trousseau in a room of leaves,
singing.

## STRONG HANDS

I say I'm a good man,
good as any man.
Winter, summer, I can tell the time by the light,
walk the road for fourteen hours.
See. Strong hands.
I stink like an old dog fox
but I'm good as any man.

I gave the girl a roof above her head
and she stole milk from me.
I cleared the dog dirt down at the track
and the boys sent me into the hedge
for a box of food.
Tricking bastard. Shits.
A nest full of wasps and I'd seventy stings.
No wonder I dream.

I can show you the scar
where they had my stomach out when Irene went,
the bitch. I'd hang her from that branch
with my bare hands. No.
Dig a pit. Kick her down.

I'd not do that to a dog. Or a cat.
I'd not do that to a fly.
I'm a good man.

I ran with the fox, old devil.
Did you see that?
Over the gardens, along at the back.

They said in the Kwik Save
I stink like an old dog fox.
*You're barred. You're barred.*
You're not the fucking Queen, I said,
you're a shit, and the day they cut off the gas
I wiped my arse on their letter
and sent it back.
I'm just as good a man.

I'll do your garden,
do your garden for you now.
See. Strong hands.

# Nick Drake

IN MEMORY OF VINCENT COX
(*born Lambeth 1923, died Harpenden 1991*)

*(for Iain Cox)*

Who loved the knack of luck, of stakes and odds,
an ace, seven sevens, a hole in one;

who disappeared on Saturday afternoons
through the forbidden ribbon door

of the obscure betting shop, to reappear
hours later in his old leather armchair,

smiling his winnings, smoking, drinking tea
by the potful, and watching the TV.

Who loved to fly, Lancasters, a bomber's moon
on midnight raids, on Dresden in '45,

the figurine homes, churches, the platz and parks
razed, each family walking shades

where china turned to ash, and tears to salt,
glass buckled, light went blind, the phosphorus heart

crazed; who still came home against the odds
in a plane he called Mizpah ('In God we Trust').

Who traded his wings in post-war civvy street
for a wife and son, the green-belt, a salesman's car

and business travelling north to Staffordshire's
bleak pottery furnaces and crucibles;

who loved the lucent angles and singing rim
of cut-glass fluted on the blowing rod

from a bulb of light; sand, potash, lime,
oxides and carbonates, transfigured to

an affluence of decanters and services,
pastoral figures on the mantelpiece,

an attic of first editions packed in straw
for his after-life, and two porcelain

lucky angels cool in his left hand
as the right turned aces up or cast the dice.

Who watched with us on winter afternoons
the Sunday war film, equally black and white;

clipped, self-effacing, nonchalant braveries,
one engine spluttering, impossibly

homing on a wing and a prayer
to the orchestra's finale and dawn's light.

Who crash-landed in his armchair, years later,
the guilty survivor when his wife had gone

and neither luck nor prayer could win her back;
whose photograph would never speak, however

long he stared, sat in the early dark
among unwashed teacups and full ash-trays

losing the slow day's games of Patience.
Who carefully washed the cups, tidied the house,

smoked his last cigarette, pencilled a note
on the back of an envelope, and then

bailed out of the attic's small trap-door
into the hall's sudden January light.

Who played the joker, but who was not this;
the undertaker's mistaken parting

running through his hair on the wrong side,
a cotton smile on his face as if he might

rise to greet us, Lazarus at his wake,
and still believe himself to be blessed by luck.

Whom I last remember as a window ghost
in his living room reflected in the night

on an incandescent lawn of December frost,
ironing his white shirts in an empty room.

Whose older brother told a better winter's tale;
White City dog track, winter '33;

mother, the infamous gambler who seems
to have wagered and lost her husband in a bet,

was having a run of bad luck, but staked her last
(their return tube fare) in a four-dog race

on the outside track; gates up,
the inside three collide and knock each other cold,

while Outside Chance raced on under the lights
to an illuminated victory

at hopeless-to-one; which brought for Wally and Vince
a slap-up tea and a taxi home to bed.

Who was released out of a winter day,
his secrets, wishes and excuses turned to ash

while we stood in his absence, uncertain
tick-tack men signing *goodbye, goodbye*

to a lucky man who seemed to lose himself
and his laughter; a chancer of odds, grounded,

who loved to fly, the navigator
over enemy country, charts and compasses,

flight angles and lucky angels, blessed wings,
seeking the constant, simple, bright North Star

in the night sky he knew by heart.
Iain, do you remember how we'd play

for coppers or matchsticks when we were kids,
your father deftly shuffling the pack?

Who might forgive – with the grace of his good luck,
with the ghost of a chance – these words as my low stake

raised against loss and in his memory,
though I can find no words to say to you.

## THE SINGLE SHOES OF SPAIN

The bridge is the gypsies' ceiling; every summer
they travel to the stones of this dry river
with the rag and bone of all the family
and set up residence, no door, no key.
The men stand at the bar; the women wash
the clothes, and lay them out on a thorn bush
or the hot stones, then retire to the shade
to watch them dry. They have no money; trade
is what the river gives away, the scrap
the wealthy town dumps off the bridge. Cars drop
broken on the rocks; cookers, burnt out,
a red armchair, some prams, a plastic bucket,
a doll's head, an umbrella. And the shoes,
the single shoes of Spain, those mysteries
of slipper, boot, stiletto without a pair,
useful only to the lottery-ticket seller
with two left feet, or a dancer with one leg;
eyes lacking laces, soles all broken tongues.
September, they move on to the winter bridges,
leaving some shoes, and several empty fridges.

# Christopher North

## THE DOG

I called amazon dot com and entered 'Robert Frost';
his hoary name a birch tree in a disco amid the graphics.
Working down the list I spotted the cassette tapes
and bounced my electric order off the satellite to Seattle.
They arrived shrink wrapped from their traverse
of the North Pole in the belly of a Boeing
and I took them on the M25 to Chelmsford.
Passing Potters Bar, with St Albans Cathedral
a squat blue bedstead on the west horizon
I listened to 'Death of a Hired Man',
the tape unspooling that ponderous conversation.
Then just before the tunnel with ceiling tracer sodiums:
'Trees at my window, window tree, my sash is lowered.'
and behind and beyond the raspy, old man's voice,
a faint dog bark out in the Massachusetts night.
It couldn't be caught, wouldn't be edited out;
barking at house lights maybe or a passing car
or rustlings from the shadows at the end of a yard,
defiant animus behind a mesh of wires.

# Hard Times

Sir,

I have removed the peacocks.
In your stewardship the mare
received an ulcered leg,
the gelding developed a cough
and the foal was undersold;
(they have a good eye for a steal
at Appleby market).
You maintain in your possession
a box of rosettes, my helmets
and all the tack room contents.

The poultry was undersold:
five bantams and a lively cockerel
should demand more than a pittance.
I wish to be advized as to the resolution
of the wheelbarrow problem:
I think you know what I mean.
It seems my books
have been all but given away.

I do not and never have
owned the freehold of Theresa Cottages;
I am merely the landlord's agent and keyholder;
kindly render up said keys forthwith.
The chaise longue is covered with mildew.
According to the experts
the chandeliers have been mishandled.
I do not wish to retain the fox mask;
you may keep it in your store
and dispose as you see fit.

I suspect and see corruption in all this
and I am writing to the Lord Chancellor.

Yours cordially

# Christiania Whitehead

What Thomist conceit saw them flaying
for balance on the head of a pin? That's
not right at all. The muscles in their
iridescent wings would be snagged
and their strong energies sapped by
such dry Latin games.

They're better in a garden. Gaining in
height and beauty even as we look.
Keeping pace with Rilke's comments
about radiance and terror, but full
also of a childlike reticence about
their errand, as they disappear behind
the topiary and re-emerge, their lips
obstinately tight,

passing the time of day anyhow.
Drumming their heels on
the tempera wattle as they loll back
and gaze abruptly into space, trying
to remember something, anything,
the suggestion of a quick task tossed
in passing over the shoulder
in that pre-picture whirl.

At last, lazily, while the girl – and we –
ache to know which flower it will be,
and which speck of soft visitation
within the womb, the miscreant
gives up his posture of absence
and attends to the task in hand. Hyacinth?
Auricula? No, it's the lily to beat all lilies
that he dabs gently from the soil
and turns on the diagonal, mounting
the steps before that outdoor, non-
perspectival prie-dieu with
growing certitude and charm.

## GRIP

Your grip is still upon me, over the sea,
touching my ear with brotherliness
and refusing awe, strong with a plain

pleasure that reaches as far as it should
and then stops. I wish that someone
with a frown would slacken your strings

and send you roaring to me.
I remember an older year, shot through
with belief, when restraint was an old hen

we sent laughing from the door.
I remember being unscared by the stealthy gait
of withdrawal she displayed. I remember

the bold way I slated amor, thinking
she would fix her lovely hands on me
till the dues of a lifetime were paid.

# The Best Individual Poems

# Caroline Carver

—HORSE UNDER WATER—

*jigharzi* an me stand in de water
warm an friendly
for de world smell like snails
ooozing on hot charcoal

an *jigharzi* step wary
as tiger fish skip between his legs
an he make like he hate de coral forever

an i slip from his back   de knife in my hand
forget de electric blue an glitter of de rainbow
an wait for shark to come over de reef
as tide lifffff de water over

an soon de fin come
quiver when it see me   but it come
shark he thick between de ears if he had them i say

an *jigharzi* he snorting and heading for land
coz dis fellow mean business
an he say why you wan kill him anyway
an i say is sport man as well as supper
an impress de tourists good an good mean money

an i say trus me *jigharzi*
an de fin go out like a light as de brute turn over
an *jigharzi* say man dis fellow bes swimmer in de sea
an de rush of water push me sideways
an de teeth glitter in sunshine that come through de water
hundreds of teeth   iiiiiichin to bite me dead
an i liff de knife but it move slow
for everything cep dis killer move slow in de water
but fear drive my hand
an i slash him in de stomach
an de monster done falter ffffffalter in de water
but he turn roun anyways
and come again   kinda slow now
an i slash him in de stomach in de same place de same place de
same place de same place
till his womb come out   an his gut
for it not a he but a lady
with babies in a bag all ready to do business
but *jigharzi* he long gone for shore
for de water full of blood   clouds of blood
clouds of froth   clouds of gore
but not clouds of joy   cos it a lady

# Robert Crawford

## ZERO

Thank you for calling Heatheryhaugh Nuclear Arsenal.
If your main lust is for weapons of mass destruction
Please try our other number in Inverbervie.

On your touchtone phone jab one for details
Of bombs that kill crofters but leave brochs and megaliths standing;
Two for snug dumpsites; three for pre-owned

Atomic oddments with warranties for several years;
Four for rucksacks of fissile material;
Five will patch you through to Glencora Gillanders,

Anthrax buyer for the Loch Ness and Great Glen area;
Six for the Arsenal's renowned in-house distillery;
Seven affords highlights of our unusual safety record,

Reassuring callers we are sited in a remote location,
Though, should you wish to visit, pressing eight provides
Pibrochs from this area of comical natural beauty.

Nine connects you to our twelve-hour emergency helpline
(Not staffed on Sundays, Hogmanay, or New Year's Day).
If this extension is busy, please yell your number

So someone can ring back at a more convenient time.
Thanks again for calling H. N. A.
*Sláinte!* Do not press zero.

# Robert Minhinnick

## Twenty-Five Laments for Iraq

The muzzein voices break the night
Telling us of what we are composed:
Coffee grits; a transparency of sugar;
The ghost of the cardomom in the cup's mosque.

These soldiers will not marry.
They are wed already
To the daughters of uranium.

Sherazade sits
In heat and dust
Watching her bucket fill.
This is the first story.

Before hunger
      Thirst.
Before prayer
      Thirst.
Before money
      Thirst.
Before thirst.
      Water.

Boys of Watts and Jones County
Build cookfires on the ramparts of Ur.
But the desert birds are silent
And all the wolves of the province
Fled to the north.

While we are filming the sick child
The sick child behind us
Dies. And as we turn our camera
The family group smartens itself
As if grieving might offend.

Red and gold
The baldaquins
Beneath the Baghdad moon,
Beneath the Pepsi globe.

Since the first Caliph
There has been the *suq* –
These lemons, this fish:
And hunched over the stone
The women in their black –
Four dusty aubergines.

*My daughter*, he says,
Stroking the Sony DV Cam,
Its batteries hot, the tally light red.
*My daughter*.

But his daughter, 12, keeps to her cot,
*Woo woo wooing* like the hoopoe
Over the British cemetery.

What are children here
But olivestones under our shoes?
Reach instead for the date
Before its brilliance tarnishes.

Back and forth
Back and forth
The Euphrates kingfisher,
The ferryman's rope.

The ice seller waits
Beneath his thatch of palm,
His money running in the gutter's tilth.

Over the searchlights
And machine gun nests on Rashid Street
The bats explode like tracer fire.

Yellow as dates these lizards
Bask on the basilica.
Our cameraman removes his shoes,
Squats down to pray.

Radiant,
With the throat of a shark,
The angel who came to the hundreds
Sheltered in Amariya.

In the hotel carpark
One hundred and fifty brides and grooms
Await the photographer.
All night I lie awake
Listening to their cries.

This first dollar peeled off the wad
Buys a stack of dinars higher than my heart.

A heron in white
And a woman in black
Knee deep together
In the green Tigris.

Her two pomegranates lie beside the bed
But they have carried the child away.

She alights from the bus
In a cloud of black,
The moon and stars upon her skirt,
And painted across her breast
The Eye that Sees All Things.

The vermilion on his toenails
        Is almost worn away,
This child of the bazaar
Who rolls my banknote to a tube
And scans through its telescope
The ruins of Babylon.

Four billion years
Until the uranium
That was spilled at Ur
Unmakes itself.
Easier to wait for the sun to die.

In the Ministry of Information
Computers are down, the offices dark;
But with me in the corridor
A secret police of cockroaches.

*Moths*, I say.
*No. Look again*, she suggests.
Fused to the ceiling are the black hands
Of the children of Amariya.

        Sometimes
The certainties return:
These cushions, a pipe,
And the sweet Basran tea
Stewed with limes.

# George Szirtes

BACKWATERS: NORFOLK FIELDS
*for W.G. Sebald*

1

Backwaters. Long grass. Slow speech. Far off
a truck heaves its load of rust into a yard
next to a warehouse full of office furniture
no one will ever use, unless to stuff
some temporary room when times are hard.
Across the fields the sweet smell of manure.

We're years behind. Even our vowels sag
in the cold wind. We have our beauty spots
that people visit and leave alone, down main
arterials and side roads. A paper bag
floats along the beach. Clouds drift in clots
of grey and eventually down comes the rain.

We're at the end. It might simply be of weather
or empire or of something else altogether.


2

Empire perhaps. Chapels in the cathedral.
Old airstrips. History's human noises
still revving down a field. Clothes pegs hang
like hanged men. It is all procedural.
Resentment simmers in the empty houses.
The wind at its eternal droning harangue.

I'm wanting to mouth the word that fits the case
but it's like trying to roll a shadow from
the street where it has been sitting for years.
It will not go. You cannot wipe the face
of the clock or restore a vanished kingdom.
You feel the shape of the thing between your ears.

Your mouth is talking to the steady light
which listens to you and remains polite.


3


How beautiful the place is. Watch it hold
time still. I want you to tell me what this is,
this place at the back of beyond, in the sun
that retains its distance in a pale gold
mirror, minding its own brilliant business,
not in the habit of speaking to anyone.

Here is a man who loves cars. He has bought
a house on something very like a hill.
He fills his yard up with old cars. He mends things –
roofs, walls. He's biblical. He does not take thought
for the morrow, won't worry when he falls ill.
He goes swooping along on wielded wings,

his children unruly, his wife losing heart.
The beautiful is what keeps them apart.

4

The WI stall. Jams, flowers. White
hair scraped back in the draught of an open door.
The butcher's. He knows you by name. He calls
your name out. His chopping block is washed bright
by the morning sun. The solicitor
down the street. His nameplate. War memorials

with more names. Rows of Standleys, Bunns,
Myhills, Kerridges. Names on shopfronts: bold
reds, whites and blues in stock typography.
Names on labels tied with string to shotguns.
Names on electoral registers. Names in gold
in the children's section of the cemetery

by the railway cutting. Willows, faint blue
in the afternoon, light gently whistles through.


5

Too easy all this, like a fatal charm
intended to lull you into acquiescence.
Think karaoke. Sky. The video shop.
Broken windows. The sheer boredom. The alarm
wailing at two a.m. The police presence.
Pastoral graffiti on the bus stop.

Think back of the back of beyond 'beyond'. End
of a line. The sheer ravishing beauty
of it as it runs into the cold swell
of the North Sea, impossible to comprehend.
The harsh home truisms of geometry
that flatten to a simple parallel.

This is your otherness where the exotic
appears by a kind of homely conjuring trick.

6

A fifteen-eighties mural. A hunting scene
runs right around the room. A trace of Rubens,
Jordaens, a touch, even, of Chinese
in the calligraphic lines. Experts clean
the powdery limewash, two PhD students
from the university, anxious to please.

A strange dome appears, out of period
somewhere near the top. Even here
there's something far flung in the code
of a different language, another God
extolling other virtues, a pioneer
morality just waiting to explode.

Flemish brickwork. Devastation. Riders
exploring hidden walls with snails and spiders.


7

You're out at the end of the pier. It is winter.
Tall waves splutter underfoot. Gulls pirouette
and dive into dark grey. The radio is alive
with music. Its tiny voices seem to splinter
into sharp distinct consonants. You forget
the time of day. It's someone else's narrative

buzzing beneath you. New explorers come
out of the light to exploit the heart of darkness.
The world is inside out, exposed as never before.
Water and sky are a continuum.
A terrible gaiety rustles the sea like a dress
it must discard. It sweeps by just once more

then drops across the beach and remains there
in the memory, in ghosted, mangled air.

8

How beautiful it is, this silence waiting
on salt. The disused railway lines between
wild blackberries. The faint hum of stray flies
on windowsills. Time is accelerating
down the coast road leaving behind a clean
pair of heels and a whiff of paradise.

The man with welded wings roars past, in love
with reason. His wife leaves in a freak gust,
their children flying along. Dogs race across
the walls in search of a lost treasure trove.
Gently idling, vast trucks deposit rust
in empty yards with patches of dry grass.

Broad fields out of town. The slow unravelling
of a long reel where everyone is travelling.


9

Travelling through or ending. The damp house
beyond the library where an old woman
has been retreating for some fifty years,
and still retreats towards a dangerous
blind alley, towards a corner, where the nearest demon
might swallow her up leaving no more tears.

There are none left to shed in the overgrown
garden with its coarse weeds. It is as if
she had been sleeping a century or more,
without a retinue, simply on her own,
growing ever more querulous, ever more stiff
till rigor mortis had frozen her four score

into zero. Country aristocracy.
The dead fields at their last-gasp fantasy.

## 10

A place full of old women. Hardy, courageous,
muttering to themselves and others in cafés,
engaging unwilling partners in conversation,
accosting young men, making outrageous
advances to middle-aged couples with tea-trays,
embarrassing husbands with their ostentation.

Old men in betting shops peering to check
the odds. Old men, natty in white, creaking
over bowls, with Beryl Cook elegance.
Old men tottering, sticking out a neck
at the neighbour while the latter is speaking.
Old men in the church hall learning to dance.

The old in their gerontopolis. At home
in sheltered housing, under the pleasure dome.


## 11

How many times do I have to say the word: End!
and still not end. You can't go further than
the sea, not on a motorway. And what
are you doing here, yes, you and your friend
from Morocco, Uganda, St. Kitts or Pakistan?
Whatever has brought you to this far, flat

kingdom with its glum farmers! Surely you
don't think this is America where dreams
are the given, where you swear allegiance
to a new self? Have you somehow fallen through
the net of the world to be lost among reams
of legislature in these alien regions?

Homing. We are homing to the sea. Back
where we never were, at the end of the track.

## 12

On a high-cloud day, you could drown in sky
round here. You see the gentle swaying
of leaves along a wall. Something under
the water, under the sky-light, in the dry
cabin under the ocean is quietly playing
a music of muted bells in soft thunder.

It is eating you away until you've gone,
like the spider scurrying up its own spit
back to its natural centre in the dark.
And the sky remains enormous. Someone
is watching the house-martin, the blue tit,
the tiny insects making their tiny mark

in the grass, and the small rain that falls far
across the field as on a distant star.

# R S Thomas

BLACKBIRD

Its eye a dark pool
in which Sirius glitters
and never goes out.
Its melody husky
as though with suppressed tears.
Its bill is the gold
one quarries for amid
evening shadows. Do not despair
at the stars' distance. Listening
to blackbird music is
to bridge in a moment chasms
of space-time, is to know
that beyond the silence
which terrified Pascal
there is a presence whose language
is not our language, but who has chosen
with peculiar charity the feathered
creatures to convey the austerity
of his thought in song.

# The Other Poems

# Annemarie Austin

SWADDLED

Swaying still on the hook
after the hurried act of hanging,
the swaddled child looks down,
mild-eyed, on the passage-room

of dark-brown panels and a plain chair
slightly skewed. Her heart ticks slow
and breathing does not stir her bandages.
Her limbs are shut away

in a coffin-outline bundle.
Light walks upon the linen.
The nurse has left her here, for safety
for a second. Chrysalis in a cobweb.

# Matthew Barton

## THE GULF VETERAN'S WIFE DOESN'T FORESEE A LOT

I jump-start him at least once a night.

Lie there, not listening so much
as driving him through towards dawn.
My ears tune to the strain
of the grinding gears of his breath.

I shift in and out of sleep,
sometimes wake and can't pull
off the dark to see whether he's still
alive or not. I steal my hand over
the beached whale of his breast,

rest it there to feel
the vestiges of rise and fall,

the soft down. And dream…

last night I was balancing
pyramids of apples on a shelf,
they kept collapsing, however carefully
I placed each one, smacking to the ground.
And each bruised one I lifted turned
to pulp and liquid in my hand…

then leap up
under the closed lid
of silence, get astride him, ride
his solid chest.

O breathe. O my God. O like

moving a mountain, until
he splutters back into life,
my sweet engine, my love.

Then we lie there. Just breathe
as light wears away the curtain to threadbare
transparency, and the birds start up –

join our sounds: his undertone
of stones the ocean sucks,
my surface sob and shhhh…

# John Burnside

## THE ASYLUM DANCE

At one time, I looked forward to the dance:
wandering back and forth in the quiet
heat of an August morning,
packing the car with cup cakes and lemonade,
boxes of plums or cherries, petits-fours,
nuts and spice cakes, mousse and vol-au-vents.
At noon I would go upstairs
to wash and change
– Sunday best, a clean white shirt and tie –
while mother made her face
and fixed her hair.
It was something we did, every year,
in that backwater town,
abandoning our lawns and flower beds,
to meet the patients, out at Summerswood.
It seemed a privilege to be allowed
within those gates, and know we might return,
to see the meadows, stripped with light and shade,
the silent lake, the fallen cedar trees.
We went there for the dance: a ritual
of touch and distance, webs of courtesy
and guesswork; shifts
from sunlight into shade;
and when the patients came downstairs
to join us, smiling, utterly polite,
in new-pressed clothes, like cousins twice-removed,
they had the look of people glimpsed in mirrors,
subtle as ghosts, yet real, with the vague
good-humour of the lost.
How we appeared to them, I can only imagine:
too solid, perhaps, too easy with ourselves,
sure of our movements, blessed with a measured desire.
All afternoon we picnicked on the lawn

then danced in awkward couples to the hiss
of gramophones, as daylight turned to dusk:
a subtle exchange in the half-light; acts of grace:
townsfolk conferring the weight of a normal world,
homes in the suburbs, the brisk lives of men who can who sleep,
the practised charm of women who believe,
who wake and forget what they dreamed, and go off to work,
and wish for nothing.
Beside the patients, we were lithe and calm:
we doled out charity and easy praise
and waited for the dancing to erase
the pain in the knot of the throat, the birdlike
angle of defeat against the spine.
We loved them for the way they witnessed us,
standing in twos and threes in the waning light,
made other by the rhythm of the dance,
the pull of a larger world, and that taste on the air
of birch-woods and streams: that knowledge of ourselves
as bodies clothed in brightness, moving apart
and coming together, cooling
slowly, as the lawns and rose-beds cooled,
heat seeping out from the skin and bleeding away,
the goldenrod turning to smoke
at the fence line.
Friendships began out there, to be resumed
year after year, the difficult months between
absolved by the summer light; and once,
a love affair, of sorts: an awkward boy
finding a girl, and leading her, mock-unwilling
into the lighted circle of the dance, to venture steps
that felt like steps on ice, the floorboards
creaking, and thin as paper.
They danced less than an hour, then she was gone,
and when he went back, next morning, the nurses
turned him away.
I think of her every day, I dream her skin,
and for years I have driven out, in the August heat,

alone now, with Mother gone, and my contributions
store-bought: jars of pickles; cling-wrapped bread.
I stand by myself, excused from the solid ring
of bodies and, for minutes at a time,
I see it all from somewhere far above,
some landing in the house, some upper room:
it makes me think of pictures I have seen
of dancers – wisps of movement on a lawn
at sunset: faces muffled, bodies twined;
the figures so close to the darkness, they might be
apparitions, venturing on form,
pinewoods above the lake, a suggestion of watchers,
a gap between night and day, between light and shade,
and faces melting, one into the next
as if they were all one flesh, in a single dream,
and nothing to make them true, but space, and time.

# Sue Butler

## FOLKLORE

With the simplicity and good humour of Homer,
the same eye for concrete detail she swears
to having seen spirits, bleeding icons
and animals with speech.

As if she had been their class mate,
she speaks of Kolecishche the Traveller,
Alyosha Popovich and Polkan the Giant,
who journeyed all over the Russias,
slaying evil and drinking wine,

how one night after church, no more
than a girl, she was followed
through the larches by a drooling beast,
which laughed, demonic and evil,
flashing its amber eyes
like the swing of a paraffin lantern.

Her favourite is the bear with a lime wood leg,
who searches the villages, seeking
his lost limb, seeking the woman
who does not sleep, who sits
on his skin, cooking his flesh
into soup for her children, spinning
his fur into a blanket.

In her nineties, she has survived
those things that stole
all her children, except Sergei.

She married the beast
with the amber eyes but the Communists
shot him, three bullets, one late
November evening, his warm blood
dripping down her face, her new skirt,
the rented wall.

She blames herself
for not recognising the knock, the bear,
Kolecishche, Alyosha and Polkan,
her neighbours and the Orthodox church
for not hearing her when she called.

# Ciaran Carson

## THE WIND THAT SHAKES THE BARLEY

Once down by the Liberties, I met with Captain Wilde,
Resplendent in a dogskin coat and rabbit stole.
He wore a green carnation in his buttonhole,
And looked the very image of a fairy child.

I took him in my arms and set him in the lap
Of my kimono, all the better for to see him,
And I kissed his bonsai hands, I felt his wooden limb.
Then I undid myself, and offered him my pap.

He peeped at me from underneath his bicorn hat,
And murmured, with the voice of a ventriloquist,
*Just read my lips: the Eagle does not hunt the Gnat.*

He bit the good side of my neck. I snapped at him
With quadrupedal scissors of the Tailor's Twist,
And made of him a disembodied interim.

# Gillian Clarke

## Horse Goddess

*for Catrin*

As a child she'd canter the yard astride a stick
topped by the stuffed sack of a horse's head
haltered with knotted hemp.
She fed it apples and fists of grass.
At night she'd stable it
in a corner of her sleep.

When she grew strong, tall as her brothers,
she built a dancer from the bones of horses
from the knackers yard, scraped and bleached them,
wove them into limbs, the spine and thighs
of Atalanta running, set the scoured skull
of a horse between the shoulders –

– like the head of *Equus Caballus* brought from the thaw
of the million-year-old glacier.
She strung horse-woman from the studio ceiling,
a giantess who leaped in the bone light
and shadow-danced on walls where the sea shook,
and you heard the hoof and heart-beats of dead horses.

She slept four nights in a stable waiting
for the foal. Asleep, awake, asleep again
in the dark stall. Outside frost bit the fields.
Pond and bucket brimmed with icy stars.
In the mare the foetus drifted on its stem,
treading water in the blood-warm dark.

On the fourth night the mare began to steam,
filled the barn with sweat like the land of Dyfed
trapped in the enchantment of a mist.
The mare, lumbering through waves of labour,
licked and nuzzled inanimate things
mad with longing for her foal.

She stiffened, threw back her head
not breathing for a long moment.
Then, a hoof from the waters, a small muzzle
shaking itself with a sneeze out of the caul,
slipped flipping like a landed fish,
first footing into the world.

# Marcia Douglas

## ELECTRICITY COMES TO COCOA BOTTOM

Then all the children of Cocoa Bottom
went to see Mr. Samuel's electric lights.
They camped on the grass bank outside his house,
their lamps filled with oil,
waiting for sunset,
watching the sky turn yellow, orange.
Grannie Patterson across the road
peeped through the crack in her porch door.
The cable was drawn like a pencil line across the sun.
The fireflies waited in the shadows,
their lanterns off.
The kling-klings swooped in from the hills,
congregating in the orange trees.
A breeze coming home from sea held its breath;
bamboo lining the dirt road stopped its swaying,
and evening came as soft as chiffon curtains:
Closing. Closing.

Light!
Mr. Samuel smiling on the verandah –
a silhouette against the yellow shimmer behind him –
and there arising such a gasp,
such a fluttering of wings,
tweet-a-whit,
such a swaying, swaying.
Light! Marvellous light!
And then the breeze rose up from above the trees,
swelling and swelling into a wind
such that the long grass bent forward
stretching across the bank like so many bowed heads.
And a voice in the wind whispered:
Is there one among us to record this moment?
But there was none –

no one (except for a few warm rocks
hidden among mongoose ferns) even heard a sound.
Already the children of Cocoa Bottom
had lit their lamps for the dark journey home,
and it was too late –
the moment had passed.

# Pamela Gillilan

## THREE WAYS TO A SILK SHIRT

You have to kill for silk
and it's not easy. Those chrysalides
make themselves so private
in their tight shuttles, so safe
that they can dare to lose themselves
to metamorphosis, abandon the known body
and endure who can imagine what liquidity
before another form takes shape.

They must be murdered in the midst
of miracle, their cerements reeled off,
the long continuous thread saved
pliable, unstained, the severing bite
of the emerging moth forestalled.

The method's suffocation –
the oldest way by baking in hot sun;
but this hardens the thread,
makes unwinding a hard labour,
risks soiling by windborne dust,
is wasteful.

Steaming's another way – the plump bolls held
above a boiling cauldron for eight minutes
then for eight weeks spread out to dry
well-aired, so that the corpse in the shroud
desiccates slowly, leaves no stain;
but sometimes the chrysalis survives.

Surest is heated air. A single day exposed
to the technology of fans and ducts, the flow
of arid currents, and the pupa's void,
a juiceless chitin spindle shrivelled back
from the close wrappings drawn and spun
out of its former self – now to be unwound
and spun again: woven, dyed, cut and sewn,
collared and cuffed.

## Paul Groves

### A High Room off Spitalgasse

*In the eighteenth century, Dr Tissot told of a school in Bern*
*where a whole class masturbated during the metaphysics lesson*
*of a nearsighted teacher.*

The boys of Bern are beating their meat.
The *professeur* doesn't see them do it.
He writes on the blackboard, small and neat.
Metaphysics is driving them to it.

Down below in the busy street
a bright new morning is under way.
Here it is disciplined, discreet;
lofty parameters hold sway.

Over in Königsberg, Kant is thriving.
Leibniz is dead, but his words live on.
Hume is alive and well, and living
in Edinburgh. But here in Bern

twenty boys are cleaning their rifles,
buffing their swords, pounding their pork,
while the *professeur* is dealing in trifles,
vague abstractions, shadow talk.

Their eyes are glassy, their faces are set
in rapt attention, while under each desk
a gentle frenzy continues. Yet
all he sees is a picturesque

Spinozan equation that he alone,
among those present, can understand.
He turns, thick-lensed in his twilight zone:
"If you have a question, please raise your hand."

Reflexively, ten hands go up.
They are all left hands. He turns again
to the crowded board, to his brimming cup
of obtuse wisdom, his regimen.

# Mark Halliday

The editors of *Whang* invite poetry that wears purple
stiletto heels without claiming that this is heroic,
and red football jerseys with the numeral 88.
We expect the kind of momentum and alternating current
that you'd expect with your head in the mouth of
Sophia Loren in 1957. Please single-space and leave
visible margins and italicize foreign words.
Do not assume that to say "Barcelona" or "heart of night"
or "blue souffle" will open every door at *Whang*.
We look for poems that embrace God *because* God has failed
and not the other way around. Send only such poems
as you would choose in lieu of a cigarette before
execution by firing squad. But do not suppose
that facile verbal violence can make us gape and squirm.
We want poems that squeak with the labor of building
elastic altars, but not poems that mop and mow
upon the moony terrace, nor desiccated poems
that wring their hands above a carpet of twigs.
Strange is okay, but not So-Proud-To-Be-Odd.
If your work merely shuffles and titters
with chipmunks glimpsed teasingly in rearview mirrors,
please send it elsewhere. *Whang* is an outlet for sacred
lava. *Whang* is devoted to the nervous fingers of
the short shadowed person frowning in the bagel shop
at a book about Manhattan in the Twenties; but
this is far from the sort of poetry that is flecked
with marinara sauce and garlic amid exploding flashbulbs.
We are not complacent at *Whang*. Nor are we fixed.
We are incipient and pulsing. The world, for us,
is a vertigo of quicksand and we edit as freemasons
in the vale of Tempe, where love is only just before
the hour of quote loving unquote, and yet
your envelope won't even be opened if you think

it's merely a matter of boom image boom image boom image
boom. You have to care *more*. For us the dreamer is
a quincunx of trees in a gale of ink with a grace
as of owls that are not mere birds. For further guidelines
send nine dollars. If you are a churl, do not submit,
but do subscribe. We stay up late, and morning finds us
crusted with homage to fickle dancers whose hair is fizzy.
If you wish your poems returned, check the alley out back.
Know this, know this, we are not just "doing our thing",
we are not just "another eccentric mag". Things have gone
way, way past that. Life whispered "spring" and we sprang.
Do not take us for granted at *Whang*.

# Sophie Hannah

## NEXT DOOR DESPISED

Next door despised
your city. They would much prefer a town.
Your tree – they'd like a twig.
Your oil rig,
your salmon satin crown,
so can you cut it down and cut it down?

Next door began
a harsh campaign. They hired a ticket tout
to sell your oily tree,
your haddocky
crown for a well of drought,
and then they bricked it up and shut it out.

Next door perceived
an envelope was lying on your stoop
but no one wrote to them
so your silk hem
deserved their mushroom soup.
Next door made plans to follow you to group

therapy, pinch
your problems, change their characters and looks.
Next door alleged your streams
gave them bad dreams.
Couldn't you call them brooks?
Couldn't you write some better, shorter books?

Next door observed
your shoulder stump, asked what was up your sleeve,
swore that they meant no harm,
said that to arm
dictators was naïve
(no pun intended). Next door don't believe

you've gone to work,
neither the place nor the activity.
While next door's squirrel slipped,
your manuscript
lolled on the balcony
which might seem natural to you or me

but to next door
it was a gate wide enough to admit
the dwarves in overcoats
who chase weak votes,
whose coffee smells of shit,
whose stubble shakes only when candle-lit.

Next door have got
their own house but they choose to squat in yours.
If you brought up their theft
of what was left
and asked whose ceilings, floors
and walls these were, next door would say next door's.

# Ian Harrow

BIOGRAPHICAL

My mother was born in Bamburgh
   Northumberland, where she is buried.
The vicar spoke as if they had been acquainted.
The graveyard of St Aidan's lies open to the sea
And on the village side
Rooks are scraping their harangue on northern air.
An only child
Who fell out with her father
For reasons that have not come down to us.
He was in the plumbing business
   ex-Black Watch (Boer War);
It's not clear why the villagers
Put out flags
When he departed for Seahouses.
He had women-trouble, at eighty;
There was a whisper that he died
   on the way to a recital
And that his paramour
Dropped the corpse off at a friend's
Promising to return after the performance.
His grave is somewhere in Northumberland.
As for my father's people
They died young as did he.
There are a few stories about him
Some of which are part of mine
Though he never knew me except as a boy.

# David Hart

Sheep on the line before Bucknall, I'm afraid, Sir,
one dead sheep,
then the wheels were slipping, metal against metal.
We had a woman sick before Dolau, had to wait there
for the ambulance, one young woman.

But we have come at last into the heart
of God's own country
and I have relished the anticipation,
haven't you, Sir? Two days ago, signal failure
on the single line, the up and the down waiting,
and the phone crackling. I had to put a dog off

last week at Pen-y-bont, it had joined the train
somehow alone, barked and whined pitifully
until an old lady in pink drew my attention
to the poor, big, scruffy, lovable thing.
                    I put it off into the care
of a farmer an old man on the train knew there.
We had to wait while he was fetched.

At Craven Arms one day a man on the station
demanded we wait
until he had finished a poem. Gwyn, driving,
looked at me as much to say, 'Daft bugger',
but I had to be sympathetic, didn't I?
                    I explained over the intercom
that we had 'operating difficulties'. Gwyn,
over a coffee later, said I'd wait for a butterfly
to hatch from its chrysalis at Ffairfach
if it wanted to travel. I said, 'Maybe I would'.

These memories will blur, Sir, there will be good days,
and one day I shall retire by the sea,
I shall alight at the end of the line
and never get back on it. My whole life late.
Have a good day, Sir, take the scenic route.

# W N Herbert

FIRST FIT

*'…three times he failed to improve upon his original handwriting, and
so today the script is preserved to us in rubbings, with all the deletions
and additions as they stood in the first draft.'*
    Lin Yutang discussing 'The Orchid Pavilion' by Wang Xizhi


Wiz ut Hogmanay or the day afore?
thi fair blarin i thi daurk
an me jist staunin ootside Boots,
whaur thi Overgait yuised tae meet thi Marketgait,
waatchin thi fisses waash past
'Muzik Express' an 'Home's Break Dancer'
stoundin fit tae be
                 thi hertbeat o thi year,
birlin bairns lyk corpuscles roond,
sendin a silent clood
o doos
      tae spirl aboot
               thi City Square
and push me intae thi present.

Eh'm waatchin white bags waaltz in baldie trees
lyk some marriage atween
snaa an leaves, thi big polythene
foliage o cities. This is me *in situ*,
thi pinball afore thi shot,
wi Lin Yutang's *The Importance of Living*
in an Oxfam bag oan ma wrist,


*first fit:* first person to be met or to enter a house on New Year's Day,
considered to bring good (or bad) luck for the year; *stoundin:* pounding;
*birlin:* spinning; *spirlin:* moving in a light, lively way.

waatchin thi fisses soom past
as tho ootwith time, observin thi recurrin
wershness o hur mou, again thi slicht
slant o his ee
                    as tho these werr
the generaishuns fleein by:
that tough wee sockie wi thi stickin-plaistir
aa owre'iz fiss, as tho someone trehd tae peel'um;
thi wee fat man wi a neb lyk a low wattage licht-bulb
an black cat herr thinnin oan'iz pow; thon lass
wi the eyebrows o Nitocris an thi cough o Nicotina –
huv Eh no met thum aa afore, been marriet til thum,
hud thir bairns, intromittit wi them
in bleachin-fields and up thi closes o Coldside,
been uncled-an-auntied by thum, bullied
an brithered by thum, murdirt an touched, up an fur,
money an minny, da i thi daurk, sister still-
boarn i thi dawin, daein fur wan an doin anither –
huv Eh no been swirlin aroon thi swelchie o histry wi
ain and aa o thum, Pict & Pole & Pakistani,
Norman & Gael & Dutcher, Viking & Jew,
Northumbrian & Welsher, Roman leeins
and Armada droonlins, Eskimos oan floes
and Italians in vans: huv Eh no
been ilkane o thum hurryin thi nicht,
buyin burgirs & pehs & pittas & kebabs,
candyfloss & cola i thi cauld?

                    Naw,
that's a wee bit lyk speirin
is that no Agnes Gardner that beat up Betty Mercer
in Dundee oan November 12th 1521


*soom:* swim; *wershness:* sourness; *sockie:* someone walking with an
exaggeratedly masculine air; *neb:* nose; *intromittit wi:* had sex with;
*minny:* mother; *swelchie:* whirlpool; *leeins:* leavings; *speirin:* asking.

an hud tae pey'ur fehv shillin?
Or is that that Sandy Paterson wha complained
'certane franschmen clum ower ma zaird dykis
and tane away ma cale' in 1552?
And that fast pair in thi matchin pig-bladder blousons,
ur they no Alexander Clerke and Elesebeth Stevinsone,
banished frae thi toon fur theft and
'gryt sumptuous spending be nygcht continuandly'?
And whit aboot hur in the flooer-print lycra frae Markies,
aye, hur wi thi furst puffy bloom o vodka roond her een,
shairly she's Marjorie Schireham, customar o Dundee
atween 1326 and 1332?

                Naw, mebbe no.


There's nae solvendiness tae Dundee's screed;
uts anely alphabet is fisses and
a screel o limbs across thi pehvment's sklate:
a gashlin haund that's got thi shauky trummles,
camshauchle, haurd tae read. Uts historicals's jist
this street and thi fowk scrievat oan ut,
fleerin and fleein lyk pages burnin, ink fadin.
There's nae set text tae net a shoal o,
lyk sparlins fae thi Tay, jist thi constantly
beginnin rebrimmin o a leid,
thi crop of thi waatir, usually crappit in by laddies
or a coo, probably pollutit by a limepit,
not potable, splore-pearls o tint voices.


*customar:* collector of customs; *solvendiness:* trustworthiness; *screed:*
a length of script; *screel:* squeal; *sklate:* slate used for writing on; *gashlin:*
distorted, writhing; *shauky trummles:* nervous tremors; *camshauchle:*
difficult to repeat; *historicals:* historic documents; *scrievat:* written; *fleerin:*
mocking; *sparlins:* smelt; *leid:* language; *crop o thi waatir:* the first water
taken from a well after midnight of December 31, supposed to bring
good luck for the New Year; *splore-pearls:* drops of saliva ejected by
a speaker; *tint:* lost.

Tae even sey ye hear ut's tae mak yirsel
MacCaliban insomniac wi stations inniz fillins
that naebody else hiz ever tuned tae;
tae grant yirsel an island atween yir lugs,
a city in a whisky piggie at thi Noarth Pole.
Tae claim ye can translate ut intae script's
tae be thi year's new monstir, mair
cartoon than skrymmorie: a reid herrin-hog, mutatit,
mair like a history minnow, twa heidit in
print's pollutit Swannie Ponds;
thi recoardin angle tae thi norm,
thi mornin blackie that's hauf-worm, howkin
uts ain tail oot o thi back green o Blackness,
haalin utsel back intae thi yird.

*whisky piggie*: an earthenware container for whisky; *skrymmorie*: terrifying; *reid hog*: fish wrapped with a red ribbon, a New Year's gift; *yird*: earth.

# Michael Hofmann

## LAST WALK

The two of you, thirty-seven years married,
and only to one another, I should add –

some odd stone or metal for that, or medal –
arm in arm, old, stable (your new trick,

except at your age you don't learn new tricks,
more as if all your lives you'd understudied

age and stability), me buzzing round you
like an electron, first one side then the other,

the long walk by the concrete-bedded river,
the Sempt, whose tributaries arrive in pipes,

the heavy July whiff of river and linden,
low water, weeds, a few fish,

the ducks beside themselves at nightfall,
the unfailingly noisy dog and cherished for it,

the last remaining farm in the new suburb,
*alteingesessen*, a hayfield among garden plots,

all the way up to the quarry pool,
the gigantic activity of the new airport

racing day and night to completion like a new book,
and somewhere in it all, your tenderness

for a firefly.

# Jackie Kay

## CROWN AND COUNTRY

When you come to our country
you will realise we are big on dentistry:
at the border your mouth will be opened, flossed
and an elegant silver filling stamped into D10.
Then you will catch the hygienic autobus, *Tooth
Fairy Express* smiling the improved smile of our people

who all know dentures are more crucial
than culture. We do not talk much, we say
cheese; pints of creamy gleaming teeth,
pouring out our white grins, our gold caps; smirks.
Just across the border, people have hellish holes,
gaping gaps, rotten roots, abscesses.

We identify people by their bite.
The lower class have most unusual bites.
They are sick to the back teeth.
At 2 a.m. on a hot dusty night in our town
you will hear the fraught percussion
of the entire population grinding its teeth.

Our dentists are the richest in the world,
mining our gobs of gold. They love the old;
the ones who finally succumb to receding gums,
to teeth falling haplessly out like hailstones.
Be careful of the wind; it can make your mouth fly wide.
All along this natural canal, you will note,
our wild poppies pout; lush red lips.

# August Kleinzahler

## Sunday Morning

How oddly content, these dogs of the homeless,
asleep at their feet in doorways, under benches,
good, healthy coats, breathing easily

Sunday morning in the fog downtown, in the quiet
as the hotels and neighborhoods awaken
to clouds of eggs and excrement, the chatter

on color TVs, spectacular reds and greens.
The ragged sleepers tremble under blankets
of newsprint, cough, turn over, curl as far

into themselves as they can, careening through
the switchbacks of dreams, fighting the wheel
as they barrel downhill, working that clutch

till the brakes go... *Oh*, with a muffled cry,
suddenly in the world like newborn babes,
except on Market, filthy and cold.

The dog opens one eye, no trouble, old routine.
Sighs and dozes off again, snoring
a thin wheezing snore, muzzle to sidewalk.

He is a well-looked-after animal,
fed as best as one can, touched, held.
The man tickles behind his dog's ear.

Fella's ear twitches. He calls him *Fella*.
That's what the guy he got him off called him.
Good, brown, short-haired mutt,

not too dumb and doesn't make a big fuss.
All of his pleasure, all that's left of love –
ridiculous tragic: 45lbs. of snoring dog.

But it's mutual, you see, and genuine.
Real as warm food in an empty belly.
And, in fact, that's just what it is for them both:

Fella's dog smell, the heat that raises it,
and that sour, musty smell the man has,
they all have, the stairwells and walls have

wherever they congregate. But Fella's friend
has his very own, very delicious smell,
a bit like old bones, urine, soup.

# Michael Laskey

## HOME MOVIES

By the final frame of the film, before
the tinny rattle of a jerked reel
or that dazzle on the bald sitting-room wall,
Dad had leaped up beside the projector

and flicked the switch, so their shaky story
went ratcheting on, only backwards now:
led in by balloons, bouncing cans and clouds
of exhaust, the car came reversing surely

far too fast at the horseshoe of guests
crowding Gran's gravel, and we had to laugh
at the way our would-be father muffed
his entrance, emerging bottom first

to pose for a moment with his right arm
flung round an untarnished version of Mum.
No sound, just a pan of everyone
cracking up, the storm before the calm

delivery by Dad of some old joke.
Hilarious how they all skedaddled
backwards up the steps into the middle
of the reception: a piece of cake

that a waitress snatched; each hopeful wish
promptly returning unopened to sender
as the knife they were forcing up together
lifted off, leaving the icing unblemished;

a quick balancing trick put the tiers in place;
then unedited longueurs – little movement,
too many self-conscious close-ups of distant
relations and friends they'd lost without trace

and whom we'd never known – nothing comical
except for a slim-line uncle Jim
brightening as glass after glass of his wine
vanished, sucked up by the mouth of the bottle.

It was round about then, while we were all
full of it, paralytic at him
sobering up, that Mum left the room
with a kind of abruptness that niggled

(or would have, if we'd adjusted our focus,
not chosen not to notice) and so she missed
what followed: their ceremonial kiss
outside the church; Dad reaching across

to conceal her face with the antique veil;
and once the blinking guests had withdrawn
into the dark doorway arm in arm
he steered her backwards, helped by two small

bridesmaids tugging her train in towards
the vestry, the moment when he'd unscrew
his pen and one by one they'd undo
their signatures, going over the words

from right to left so they disappeared,
and suddenly the twinkle in Dad's eye
was a hard gleam in the flickering light
and the rare warmth of the atmosphere

too close: not one of us raised the ghost
of a laugh as Dad softly eased the ring
off the finger so gladly held out to him,
or dared interrupt to point out the past

was spilling out, already ankle-deep
on the floor and spreading. He stood so still
we didn't exist. There was nothing real
but that slither of negatives at his feet.

# Aidan Mathews

## Total Immersion

In my second life
I want to be decanted as two atoms
Of hydrogen and one of air you can sing to.

My eager, evergreen rivers would
Fatten the lapping capitals,
The kids wade into me beyond their umbilicus.

Such cloudshapes I would stage on sabbaths,
Army convoys would stop in their trucks,
The nuncio cable Rome,

And amateur painters on *Autobahnen*,
Agog at the Tabor truth of my colours,
Forget the numbers for field-grey and azure:

I would be black and blue for them,
Yet the winter sun would pierce me through,
A laser of light, a picture of innocence.

On the benevolent I would fall as snow,
On the evil, even on Mozart's murderer,
I would settle as drizzle.

Men in the shabby bedlam of stetls,
Their foreheads grimy as anthracite miners,
Would angle their cheeks like shoolchildren

For many swift kisses. Then
in my passing, my passion, my pietà,
The world's slate would be wiped like a window.

Meantime I am happy to be
A puddle at the zebra,
Too muddy to look up anyone's underwear,

Or even a Tupperware what-you-may-call-it
Of drinking water left at a heater
To dampen down the atmosphere

And shiver at the sudden sound-waves
Of a girl in a bed-sit dropping, thud,
First one espadrille, thud, then the other.

# Roger McGough

## The Way Things Are

No, the candle is not crying, it cannot feel pain.
Even telescopes, like the rest of us, grow bored.
Bubblegum will not make the hair soft and shiny.
The duller the imagination, the faster the car –
I am your father and this is the way things are

When the sky is looking the other way,
do not enter the forest. No, the wind
is not caused by the rushing of clouds.
An excuse is as good a reason as any.
A lighthouse, launched, will not go far –
I am your father and this is the way things are

No, old people do not walk slowly
because they have plenty of time.
Gardening books when buried will not flower.
Though lightly worn, a crown may leave a scar –
I am your father and this is the way things are

No, the red woolly hat has not been
put on the railing to keep it warm.
When one glove is missing, both are lost.
Today's craft fair is tomorrow's car boot sale.
The guitarist gently weeps, not the guitar –
I am your father and this is the way things are

Pebbles work best without batteries.
The deckchair will fail as a unit of currency.
Even though your shadow is shortening
it does not mean you are growing smaller.
Moonbeams sadly, will not survive in a jar –
I am your father and this is the way things are

For centuries the bullet remained quietly confident
that the gun would be invented.
A drowning Dadaist will not appreciate
the concrete lifebelt.
No guarantee my last goodbye is au revoir –
I am your father and this is the way things are

Do not become a prison-officer unless you know
what you're letting someone else in for.
The thrill of being a shower curtain will soon pall.
No trusting hand awaits the falling star –
I am your father, and I am sorry,
but this is the way things are.

# Andrew Motion

## SERENADE

There were the two ponies – that was one thing –
and then there was Serenade, which belonged
to my mother. Though "who belonged" would be better
than "which belonged", in view of that girlish head-lift

and flounce to and fro in the lumpy field she had,
and that big womanish rump I always gave a wide berth.
When the blacksmith came to shoe her, which was not much
in summer, but otherwise often, she would let him lift

and stretch out first one hind leg, then the other,
with a definitely melancholy, embarrassed restraint,
as though she knew her entire fangle of arsehole,
cunt, etc, which her tail generally kept out of sight,

was on display but sadly squiffed: a miniature cascade
of matt dark candle-wax, or lava which never set.
The blacksmith was ferret-faced and rat-bodied,
hardly man enough to keep aloft the great weight

of one-foot-at-a-time, though he did keep it almost
aloft, crouched over double, and bent at the knees,
to make a peculiar angle which kept each hoof still
on his battle-scarred apron. Without rhyme or reason

he would set up shop in the old coveted entrance-thing
between our house and the stable-block: a ramshackle
clapboard affair, black (or black weathering to green),
with swallows' mud-villages proliferating in the rafters.

Maybe he felt trapped in the small spaces of a stable
proper; I don't know. Anyway: I liked it there in the drive-
through – which was also where we parked the car,
(but not on his days) – for the oil-maps on the dusty cement

brilliant as the wet skin of a trout, and also for the puzzling
swallow-shit patterns, and most of all for that place
by the corner-drain where a grass-snake had appeared
once – an electric-green, sleepy-looking marvel

which, when it disappeared, left a print of itself
(but not really) that stayed in place for ever.
The blacksmith always did cold shoeing, prising off
each old moon-crescent, if that was the job in hand,

then carving the hoof with a bone-handled,
long-bladed knife. The miracle of no pain!
Serenade gone loose in her skin, her strength
out of her, so she seemed suspended in water,

her hypnotised breathing steady, the smell of piss and musty hay
and ammonia sweat coming off her,
and her head dropping down, eyes half closed now,
and me a boy watching the earth-stained sole of her hoof

turning pure white as the blacksmith pared and trimmed,
leaving the nervous diamond of the frog well alone
but showing me, just by looking, how even to touch that,
much worse cut it, would wake her and break the spell

and then our two heads with it. Our collie dog sat near
where the snake had been, ravenous black and white,
all ears, sometimes fidgeting her two slim front feet,
glancing away as if about to dash off, then looking back,

licking her lips and swallowing with a half-whine.
She knew better than to get under anyone's feet,
but when the blacksmith had done with his cutting,
and offered a new shoe, and fiddled it a bit if that

was what was wanted, and hammered it with quick hits
which drove the nail-points clean through (but these
could be filed off later, and were) – when this was all done,
he kicked the clippings any old how across the cement

and then it was the collie's turn to show a sad restraint,
taking one delicate piece between her pink lips, ashamed
to be a slave of appetite, and curving away into the yard,
to eat it in private. The blacksmith straightened himself,

one hand soothing the small of his back, the other picking
a few remaining nails from between his own darker lips –
which reminded me of my mother when she was sewing,
her mouth thoughtful or even spiteful – not meeting my eye,

but slapping Serenade on the flank with his red palm,
rousing her from her trance, running his fingers up
her mane and over her ears, giving each a soft tug,
and saying "She'll do", or "Good lady", or "There's a girl".

Whereupon my mother herself appeared to pay him –
I mean, their hands met, and touched, and parted,
and something passed between them – and the blacksmith
took off his apron, with its colours of a battered metal bowl,

folded it, and carried it slowly before him in a lordly fashion,
using it as a cushion for his collapsed bag of hammers,
knives, files, pliers, nails and such-like, to the van
which he had parked in the lane some distance from us,

while my mother untied the halter and led her horse away.
There was a crisp cocoa-nut clip-clop over the stable yard,
and a train of hoof-prints with the neat shoes obvious to me,
who had stayed behind with nothing better to do than look.

This was Serenade, who would later throw my mother
as they jumped out of a wood into sunlight, and who,
taking all possible pains not to trample her down, or even
touch her, was nevertheless the means to an end, which

was death. Now I am as old as my mother was then,
at the time of her fall, and I can see Serenade clearly
in her own later life, poor dumb creature nobody blamed,
or could easily like any more either, which meant nobody

came to talk to her much in the place she eventually took up
under the spiky may tree in the field, and still less
came to shoe her, so her hooves grew long and crinkled
along the edges like wet cardboard (except they were hard),

while she just stood there not knowing what she had done,
or went off with her girlish flounce and conker-coloured arse,
waiting for something new to happen, only nothing ever did,
beyond the next day and the next, and one thing leading to another.

# Les Murray

## TRAVELS WITH JOHN HUNTER

We who travel between worlds
lose our muscle and bone.
I was wheeling a barrow of earth
when agony bayoneted me.

I could not sit, or lie down,
or stand, in Casualty.
Stomach-calming clay caked my lips,
I turned yellow as the moon

and slid inside a CAT-scan wheel
in a hospital where I met no one
so much was my liver now my dire
preoccupation. I was sped down a road

of treetops and fishing-rod lightpoles
towards the three persons of God
and the three persons of John Hunter
Hospital. Who said We might lose this one.

Twenty days or to the heat-death
of the Universe have the same duration:
vaguely half an hour. I awoke
giggling over a joke

about Paul Kruger in Johannesburg
and missed the white court stockings
I half remembered from my prone
still voyage beyond flesh and bone.

I asked my friend who got new lungs
How long were you crazy, coming back?
Five days, he said. Violent and mad.
Fictive Afrikaner police were at him,

not unworldly Oom Paul Kruger.
Valerie, who had sat the twenty days
beside me, now gently told me tales
of my time-warp. The operative canyon

stretched, stapled, with dry roseate walls
down my belly. Seaweed gel
plugged views of my pluck and offal.
The only poet whose liver

damage hadn't been self-inflicted,
grinned my agent. A momentarily
holed bowel had released flora
who live in us and will eat us

when we stop feeding them earth.
I had, it did seem, rehearsed
the private office of the grave,
ceased excreting, made corpse gases

all while liana'd in tubes
and overseen by cockpit instruments
that beeped or struck up Beethoven's
Fifth at behests of fluid.

I also hear when I lay lipless
and far away I was anointed
first by a mild metaphoric church
then by the Church of no metaphors.

Now I said, signing a Dutch contract
in a hand I couldn't recognise,
let's go and eat Chinese soup
and drive to Lake Macquarie. Was I

not renewed as we are in Heaven?
In fact I could hardly endure
Earth gravity, and stayed weak and cranky
till the soup came, squid and vegetables,

pure Yang. And was sane thereafter.
It seemed I'd also travelled
in a Spring-in-Winter love-barque of cards,
of flowers and phone calls and letters,

concern I'd never dreamed was there
when black kelp boiled in my head.
I'd awoken amid my State funeral,
nevermore to eat my liver

or feed it to the Black Dog, depression
which the three Johns Hunter seem
to have killed with their scalpels:
it hasn't found its way home,

where I now dodder and mend
in thanks for devotion, for the ambulance
this time, for the hospital fork lift,
for pethidine, and this face of deity:

not the foreknowledge of death
but the project of seeing conscious life
rescued from death defines and will
atone for the human.


The three eponyms of John Hunter Hospital, in Newcastle New South
Wales, are respectively the Scottish pioneer of modern surgery, the
Scottish second Governor of NSW after whom the city's river is named,
and the youngest-ever Professor of Medicine at Sydney University,
appointed at 24, dead of typhoid at 26, in the nineteen twenties.

# Stephanie Norgate

## THE WHEEDLING MAN

Just because he spoke in a wheedling sort of way,
just because he looked ashamed and afraid,
just because he whined and crouched,
just because he was so aware of his lost life,
fingering the old bus-pass in his pocket,
the photograph of his wife, just because
he drew his jacket round him against the cold
even though it was a warm blue day,
just because he puckered his face and looked like he might cry,
or suddenly piss on the venerable paving stones,
just because he wouldn't let up, was desperate
and sad, I didn't give him anything.
And now it's no consolation
to the hungry wheedling man, that he's stayed in my head
and won't go away, that I can replay every word of what he said,
how he looked; that I'm still walking down the lovely old alleyway
with its famous trace of an open sewer,
swishing my feet in gold-fingered horsechestnut leaves,
thinking of this man I meet everyday at four for sex,
(but no so crudely as that, in a kind of haze)
when he gets up from under the wall and approaches me,
his voice whining in my ear, his tweedy jacket
brushing my shoulder,
*please love love please love spare me some change*
dancing in front of me, stopping me getting on.
But two hours earlier, a man
with matted hair and Rasputin eyes
said to me firmly, 'I need two pounds. Give it me.'
And I gave instantly.

# Bernard O'Donoghue

## HERMES

*And now I long to be a poet/With something good to say.*
    (i.m. Denis O'Connor, 1918-97)

Just as I'm happier walking in the dark
Of night and feel more safe in planes
Than on the ground, I'm less at ease
Among the living than the dead.
For years I've specialized in writing
Letters to the bereaved, a brief
From a licensed afterlife, consoling
Children, widowers and widows.

But who am I to write to you about you,
Denis, who made your own way? I'd like
To honour your unrivalled singing,
Your melojeon, and your wit-barbs;
Your merriment among the dancers,
And your vamped mouth-organ. Who do I remind
How you could run up the twenty rungs
Of a ladder standing in the middle
Of the yard, our stilted boy?

You had the excitement of the hare,
And a like form, away from the everyday.
You had the fox's glamour, the perfectly
Made out-of-the-ordinariness
Of that thrush's nest, sealed with spit,
You showed us above the arum lilies.
We admired, but didn't understand
That you were Hermes, bearing messages
From the past, and must return, like summer
Out over the top of the fairy-thimbles.

Who dug your grave, Denis,
Since you dug everyone's?
Who carried your coffin?
There's no one in the parish
Who would not push to the front
Of the crowd to bear you.
Are we now at liberty to call you
Dansel, the venerated, unaccounted-for
Nickname of your family,
That no-one spoke in your presence –
Out of some sentiment: tact? or fear?
Love maybe. In the silence
After your death, may we speak it now?

In the grave, shall all be renewed?
Your celebrity? Will this letter do?
No: by way of postscript I remind us all
Of a late-December night when you were old
And sick and looking for a drive
To help you get your messages up home.
It wasn't easy to make out what
You were mumbling, with the drink.
"Christmas is the worst time of all
For the person living on their own."

# Pascale Petit

## FOSSILING

The fossils are packed on top of each other
like children in dormitory bunkbeds.
Their sheets are wet. Nurses rub their noses in them.
It's the weekend, but my mother doesn't visit.

The gale is slapping me – the mother
who doesn't wish me to see her face
who had moods like this weather –
half the sky is on fire, half raining hailstones.

Between the undercliff and incoming tide,
giant ammonites are embedded in ledges
– a stone book with pages that take years to read,
stories of snakestones, devil's toenails…


This is just how it was, the slow petrification,
my core surrounded by a many-chambered shell
where I vacated rooms of selves.
The ocean pressing against my forehead.
The playground cruised by armour-plated fish.

Somewhere on the surface, a gale attacked me.
I felt nothing. The seas retreated,
were replaced by layers of stone seas.
Through cracks in the lias, voices filtered down.

Houses made of sand, shale, marl,
towerblocks, terraces, crushed together
and underneath, the ancestral house of mud.

The balcony fell into the sea
and there were floors where children were stranded,
floors so boggy we had to stay in bed,
knowing that when the voices upstairs
were raised, quicksands could swallow a child.

Bone-beds, shell-beds, stone-beds,
sheets cold as the skins of marine reptiles.

I sleepwalked down the coiled corridor,
passed doors leading to guardians' homes
– parents made of pyrite.

My thoughts were trapped in amber.
I began the long transformation of matter.


A boulder breaks open, releasing fossil ferns
– seven jewelled summers, when I drew
water from the wells of my bones
to keep Gran's garden from drying.

I climbed trees from the Coal Age
– giant clubmosses, horsetails,
and beyond the garden gate –
forests of peat, of anthracite;

the hollowed trunks of petrified trees
lined with amethyst, jasper.

On the blackboard, symbols recurred –
the mathematics of change, from leaf to fire...

Firemothers with magma in their veins,
babies that calcify in the womb
born with a stone guard in their hearts.

Daughters with the shells of trilobites,
forced to sleep in Cambrian slime,
feed on the debris of seafloors;
their skeletons on the outside,
rolled into a ball.

I uncurl the spirals of fossils,
unravelling stories buried inside me,
daughters that have to swim through stone.
The deeper I dig, the harder the child.

# Peter Porter

To My Grandaughters Sweeping Spelsbury Church

It's August and hay-fever weather,
We've left the house in Summer's tether–
While you girls scamper hell-for-leather
      And climb the wall
Our adult hopes are all on whether
      We'll find the Earl.

The youthful Earl of Rochester
In this small parish church interred
Proclaims the triumph of the word,
      A true contrition,
For penitence is gravely heard
      In a patrician.

A bully, fiend and alcoholic,
A brilliant Hobbesean melancholic,
A frightened sinner, parabolic,
      Yet first and foremost
A mind which rendered apostolic
      Sad Reason's ghost.

What would we find if we, instead
Of looking pious, raised the lid
Of where he lies encased in lead–
      Memento mori?
I doubt it–when the flesh has fled
      All's nugatory.

His soul which bigotry would save
Is shrunk to copper in the nave,
A mere inscription. Thus the grave
      Keeps all in sight
And wife and son may only have
      A year's respite.

But bouncing through the door, you girls
Pounce on the verger with skirls
Of laughter, sudden whirls and curls,
      Take up his broom,
Then, like George Herbert, for the Earl's
      Sake sweep the room.

When Martha and Amelia raise
A little dust to rightly praise
The magnitude of other days,
      They're only playing–
It's Grandad's pompous paraphrase
      Which is dismaying.

Life works the other way around:
It's what George Herbert saw which wound
His metaphor into his sound–
      A parish priest,
He'd keep his ear to the ground
      This much at least.

So give the verger back his broom
And let the Earl sleep out his doom,
I must return to London soon
      And you to Rome–
Though you're not Catholic, you assume
      There God's at home.

Is Oxfordshire more savoury
Than the ill-swept Trastevere?
Is Rome all foreign knavery?
     Our cows are mad,
Our people sunk in slavery,
     Our climate bad.

But still we speak a language which
The whole world seems to have an itch
To learn, and this may make you rich–
     England supporters–
And since you don't stray on the pitch,
     Dutiful daughters.

# Sheenagh Pugh

## THE TORMENTED CENSOR

He sees what is not given to others,
the foreign magazines before they are made
fit for the faithful. He makes them fit.

All day long, he sifts indecent women.
*Runner's World*; his glinting scissors meet
and part; amputate bare legs and arms.

All through *Hello!* his soft felt-tip is busy
stroking a chador of thick black ink
over celebrity cleavages.

Even in *Woman's Weekly*, some minx
moistens her lips with the tip of a pink tongue:
he rips it out. The whole page.

They all get shredded, the silky limbs,
the taut breasts, flesh cut to ribbons.
He is devout, and keeps none back,

but after work, walking home, if a woman
should pass, decently veiled, all in black,
his gut clenches; he tries not to look,

as the little devils in his mind whisper
what they know; melt cloth; draw curves
on her dark shapelessness.

# Peter Reading

AXIOMATIC

Man, who seldom lives a hundred years,
worries himself enough for a thousand.

Small-talk will charm a host;
straight-talk provokes dislike.

Better to die ten years early
than spend those extra years in penury.

I do not laugh at this old fart,
for I shall assuredly be thus.

Old and yellow men,
and pearls when they are yellow, are
equally worthless.

Each birthday one knows
next year will be worse.

Though we so vividly dream
of our boyhood games, our cruel mirrors
reflect snow-haired old codgers.

# Michael Symmons Roberts

## The Eel Gatherers

Beside the straight road, a disused railway track
which ferried to the front invites you to picture it then.
Beyond that, plump cows print their flanks in Flanders mud.

The eel gatherers finished here and moved
over years and kilometres to wooded valleys split by rivers,
where the lithe ones shin up trees to point out

quick black spasms in the water,
mimicking life's microscopic frenzy,
while the knee-deep scoop them into coracle baskets,

pull them from their blind instinctive journey
– Sargasso, Gulf Stream, Atlantic, then silvering upriver –
into a desperate cross-weave of each other.

# Adam Thorpe

## Pickings

Our ogres' steps of earth,
dug, yield a trove

of what they used to chuck:
keys stuck in rust's lock,

lots of bits of pot,
jabs in glass for goats

and knobs for doors long shut
from hands; each clink is luck

or a stab of sharp loss.
Jaws laid as if meant,

hips like open wings,
the lead weight of a wine

glass, snapped at the neck.
Tins, the tines of forks,

light francs from the war,
each worth what we find

to say about it; words
strung back to phrase a dream

lost like the old dame
who lived here when *le maire*

was a boy (who'd see her
propped in the dark door

with a bowl of gruel, a grin),
laid to rest just where

we light up all these things.
'She's much too deep,' I say –

my kids in hope she'll rise
one day, tucked on a spade,

like the small flask I earthed
once but did not break

marked Prix 3 Frs,
*'La Miraculeuse'*.

# Jeffrey Wainwright

## The Humane House

*'It is desirable that a man be clad so simply
that he can lay his hands on himself in the dark'*

At a knot-hole, looking inwards, ocean, land,
Beach and sky, everything outer, behind us,
If we watch faithfully we will see at length
Some wandering beam dawdle upon a shape within.

Thus Thoreau, walking one day along the Cape,
Beside the sea that comes ashore so
Indecorously, retreated from its inhuman tucks and turns
To seek and even enter that 'long-wished-for insight'.

So creased is his eye-socket against the grain,
He must believe that it is there: rolled round,
Concealed in the metaphor of a house for castaways,
Waiting on a patch of lamp-glass, the scratch on a tin plate.

Unless, as he watched, he felt a sand-grain cross his eyeball,
Sensed as he stood the contrition of all those
Unfleshed carcasses drive under the door and past the window-
    frame,
Filling the house, chasing apart the tinier and tinier

Crossways of light until they are holed up
And drowning between the close-fit slopes of sand,
Suffocated beneath a run-away now of beach and sky,
The last of light dragged first from our dwarfish sun

Then from the millions of suns still left,
Hoppered through the chimney, sucked through clapboard cracks
To be so crushed there will truly be nothing to see
And not even blackness to attend to.

What he had sought in an eventual gleam inside
Were 'the very bowels of mercy':
Some magnanimity, trust, practicality,
A gift of straw to make a fire out of the wind.

Instead he finds himself bystander at this last
Cataract of being. He unclasps his eye,
Wedges his feet in the sand and feels for his shirt-button
And a nubbin of flesh 'twixt thumb and forefinger.

# Andrew Waterhouse

## One Day in Late Adolescence

It being suggested that I get out of myself more,
I get out of the family home and into low cloud.
A door bangs behind me and here lies North Marsh Road
and December, where the lamps have been on all day.
Adjacent, there may be a town, tidal river, power station;
but this view is cut to pavement and a Maestro browning
nicely. Also, the aged appear, trolleys pulling
them home. They breathe heavily, making their own winter.

At the crossroads I wait for a lorry dribbling sand,
then straight over past The House of Close Relations,
but I will not call being sick of myself and all others.
To the right are allotments where my father buries
something most days. Note the freshly turned earth,
hear the pigeons mumbling about the sun and spilt grain.

And now a sharp rise, up the embankment, and I look down
upon the weighty Trent, brown, see the whirlpools eating
themselves and a barge grows from the fog, slips around the bend,
bearing coal to Hull and even beyond. It disappears,
making a wake I must follow, which is where I will leave myself,
hunched and walking by a river in December,
hoping that one day I will return in human form.

# Robert Wells

1


'You must realize that I am very superficial.
I have been brought up that way – to talk
About this and that.
                              This poet oh yes,
This general oh yes.
                              Five minutes' conversation.'


I exhorted you to read 'about Indian history',
Talked of your culture'
– 'You should root yourself more firmly...'

Innocent words. You smiled at my hectoring,

And preferred the chat of the moment, the dance-floor;
To glide, leaving no wake;
                              for fixity
(You taught me how to teach you)
To crouch, trapped fugitive,
In a submission which made you gasp and moan.


2


Your fantasy of annihilation
Was a joke to me. But when the girl's straw hat
Blew down between live rails
You jumped from the platform to fetch it
As if your life
                              weighed as lightly as the hat –
And handed it back, grinning,
Moments before the train hurtled through.

Was it this brave carelessness
Put paid to the attempt
To make an accountant of you?
                            Certainly
You were no 'economist of your person'.


3


The pearl in the wine, my 'right gipsy'!

– And you kissing away
My Roman shock
                            at the improvidence.


4


A spring of failed exams, of tears;
A summer of 'could-be's', wishful hopes
While you 'sung and hopped
In meadows green' –

'And now green ice':
                            the bureaucrat's
Sleights matching yours, his guarded voice
And sly relish for the order of things;
Your passport returned, visa unrenewed,
Invalid,
        having been kept all year.

5

Tears – suddenly at the barrier
As we embraced, then uselessly
On the Terminal roof
As, unclean with fatigue, I watched
Your plane take off,
                        grow small,
Its steep thrust vanish in cloud;

And the thought
That for someone landing today
The story now beginning

Was the same story
                        over again.

# Gerard Woodward

## The Handstand Summer

We lived in a one-way street,
But that didn't stop the cars
Cheating on dark nights.
I blamed the girls

Who'd been practising
Handstands all summer,
Egging each other on
Until they could kick
Themselves into the upside
Down in one movement.

It became normal to see
Feet sway like ripened
Corn past our window
And hear the clatter
Of heels as uprightness
Regained itself.

By September there were
Formation cartwheels,
Synchronized handsprings,
And we got so used
To the summery arcs
Of young feet behind
Our television, so used
To inverted footprints up
Our flank wall
That going to sleep
I really felt I might
Wake on the lunar
Landscape of our ceiling,
And it took all my
Concentration to prevent

My tea swelling
To a brown uprising.
I considered painting
'This Way Up' across
The front of the house,
I considered posting
A wine glass
And an umbrella
At the gateposts
As reminders of the rampant.
But I wondered if even
I could get enough sense
Of the perpendicular when
I was besieged by girls
Taking the world
On their shoulders in their
Bluebottle ambitions.

What world did they
Have in mind
I wondered. I found
Myself being sweet
To them, thinking
Of a place where houses
Hung like the last leaves,
Where the ground was a deep
Lake in which we
Would never drown.